BULLETIN BOARDS

For the Whole School to Enjoy

by

Robyn Spizman

illustrated by Evelyn Pesiri

Cover design by Evelyn Pesiri

Cover by Gary Mohrmann

Copyright © Good Apple, Inc., 1984

ISBN No. 0-86653-260-9

Printing No. 98765

GOOD APPLE, INC.
BOX 299
CARTHAGE, IL 62321-0299

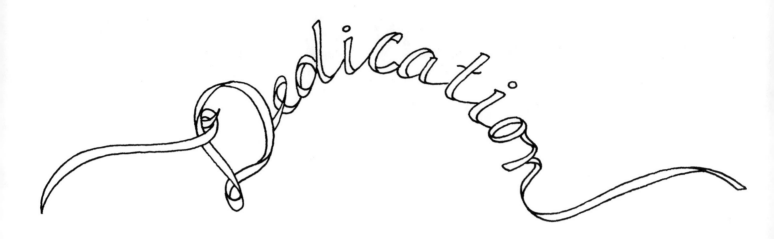

This book is dedicated to you, the teacher. It is your dedication and commitment to teaching that creates the key ingredient for making the world for children a better place to be.

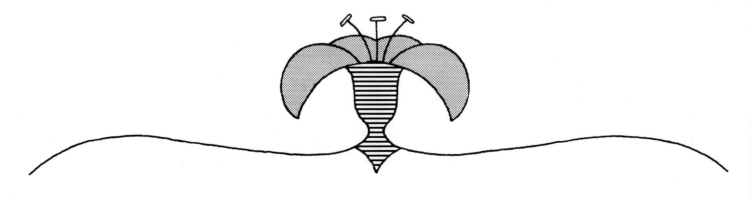

TABLE OF CONTENTS

INTRODUCTION

The purpose of this bulletin board book is to present to you, the teacher, an exciting collection of bulletin boards to use for the whole school. Each bulletin board is accompanied by an illustration, a clever title, and the overall purpose of the display.

The basic concept of this book is to cover each and every aspect of the school as a whole. Many of the bulletin boards can be applied to all the classes in your school, and provide a schoolwide effort for its completion. To enlarge the presented illustrations, use an overhead projector. If an opaque projector is available, you will not have to transfer the design to acetate in order to enlarge it. I have found that it is a lot easier to cut out the illustrations freehand. All you have to do is study the shapes and give it a try.

If you are able to laminate your characters and additional details, your bulletin boards can be recycled for years to come. Be sure to involve your students, as they are your best resource for creating displays. They will take great pride in adding their personal touch and gain a great deal from having participated in the bulletin board's creation.

I hope this book will be helpful and provide hours of learning for both you and the students in your school.

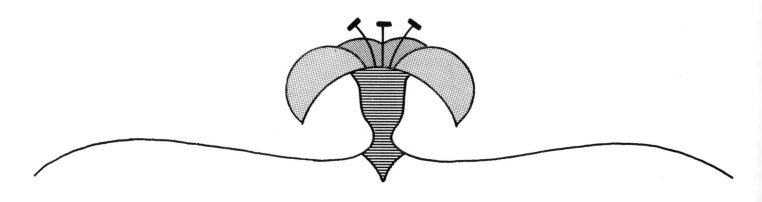

WHAT I DID LAST SUMMER

went to the zoo - Cory

went to camp in the mountains - Jared

visited Aunt Francie - Gregory

went to see my Cousin in Florida - Scott

The purpose of a graffiti bulletin board is to provide a place where students have the opportunity to express their ideas and opinions openly. Control of this bulletin board is found in the title. On this page and the following page, you will find six examples of graffiti boards and how they can be used. Using yarn and tacks, attach a variety of writing instruments to the bulletin board. Provide several types (crayon, pen, marker) and several colors. Small slips of paper can also be available. These can be placed in an envelope that is attached to the bulletin board. Students can make comments on these and then pin them to the board.

THE **GREEN SCENE**

When completing a graffiti board encourage students to write, print, draw and use pictures cut from magazines. You may wish to place a stack of old magazines near the graffiti board.

"The Green Scene" is simply a place for students to place pictures of things that are green, write in green, and list names and things that are all green. The Jolly Green Giant is green. So is the Nile (a shade of green) River, the Green Mountains, evergreen trees, wintergreen, and Mr. Greenjeans.

TO **IMPROVE** THIS **SCHOOL**

One of the most positive aspects of graffiti boards is the fact that they encourage creative thinking. Elaboration and expansion (stretching) of thought is to be encouraged.

Sometimes you may wish to limit the focus of the graffiti board. When using a topic like "To Improve This School," you may wish to ask the students to be positive in their approach. "Get rid of the principal" would not be an acceptable comment. "Provide strong administrative leadership" would be a much more positive comment.

GRAFFITI BOARDS

HEY, YOU... WHAT'S NEW?

New York!   my haircut   My new little brother ←

my puppy, Dice   my house!

Use the title above as a graffiti focus. Encourage students to be creative. Someone could write: Is Paul·Newman really new? I have a new gnu. Not everything in the newspaper is new. Television would be fairly new to a ninety-year-old man. Don't forget to include the latest fashions, crazes and the names of the current top ten records. Students could also use the dictionary to find words that contain the letters *n, e,* and *w* in order, for example, knew, renew and Newark, NJ. It is important that students have the opportunity to stretch their thinking skills. It allows them the opportunity to "use" the basic facts that they have learned. It helps them to adapt, modify and combine isolated skills and concepts.

OPINION ROUNDUP

Sometimes you may wish to focus the graffiti board on topics that are more controversial or that require students to examine their values. "Opinion Roundup" is an appropriate title. Present the question inside the lasso. Each student can print his decision or comments on a small slip of paper and attach it to the board. A conclusion or consensus need not be made. Students can view all responses and see others' opinions of the same question. A question that could be asked is: What is more important—fame, health, or wealth?

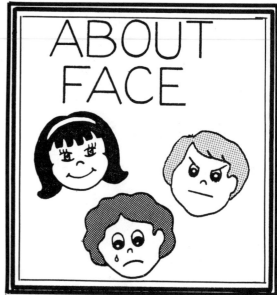

ABOUT FACE

"About Face" would be a good focus for a graffiti board. Students would simply bring in pictures of American faces. The entire area could become a montage of faces. This would then serve as a focus for several class discussions. Discussion questions could include: What does the average American look like? Is the face of America changing? Is the makeup of your community typical or do only a limited number of American types live where you live.

The titles for graffiti bulletin boards is almost limitless. You may wish to have a bulletin board like this in your room all year long. Each child could have a turn at creating the focus.

"The Lobby Hobby Bulletin Board" is one for the entire school to make, use, and enjoy. Each month a different class could be responsible for the focus. It would be that room's decision to determine what hobby should be presented. However, all rooms in the school could contribute materials, examples, and information to the bulletin board. This board should be presented in a central location where all students can see and enjoy it.

The bulletin board can also serve as a catalyst for several additional activities. The class in charge should send a notice to all other classes announcing the board and stating how others can participate in the project. A basic information sheet could also be made available to all classrooms. On this sheet there could be spelling/vocabulary words, questions, a list of resources pertaining to the focus and a list of activities to try during the month. An adult who has the focused hobby could be asked to come to school. This person could sit near the bulletin board, display items, work on a project, answer questions, and involve students who would like to be introduced to the hobby.

EXAMPLES OF HOBBIES THAT COULD BE USED:

Needlework
Suggested Title: Needlework Will Keep You in Stitches!
Description: This bulletin board could display a variety of yarns that are used in needlework. Included on the bulletin board could be tools that are used, such as knitting needles, etc., and an assortment of finished products, such as needlepoint and cross-stitch pieces.

Bird Watching
Suggested Title: Birds of a Feather Flock Together
Description: This bulletin board would introduce bird watching to students. Display a variety of birds that are commonly found in your area.

Stamp Collecting
Suggested Title: Stamp Collecting Won't Lick You!
Description: Display a variety of stamps from a student's collection. Add a pair of scissors, some letters with stamps, etc., and show how simple it is to begin this fascinating hobby.

TERRIFIC TIP: Involve your students' parents, and invite them to assist your class in this bulletin board. Many parents have exciting hobbies and would be delighted to share what they know about theirs with the class.

This bulletin board can be used to highlight your school, its history, its teachers, its workers, its philosophy, and its goals. What a great way to create positive public relations. Display in a place where all who enter your school can see. The school administrator and his staff should maintain this bulletin board. What better way for the principal to set the example that "we who work here care." Information presented could include when the school was built, its construction history, information about the school's name, a list of prominent people who attended, how many attended, the total number of hours of learning that has taken place, and other interesting facts. This bulletin board could be used to thank those whose many hours of service have made the school run smoothly.

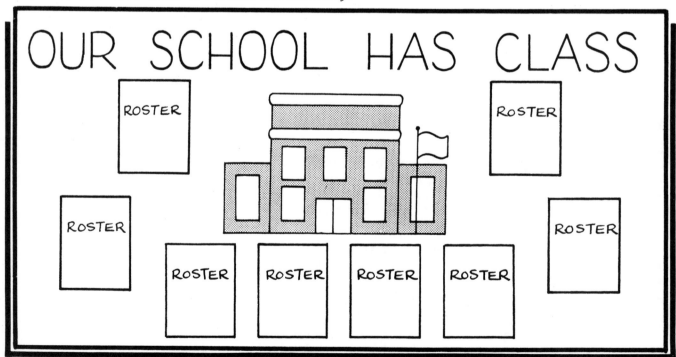

Use this bulletin board to spotlight the students in your school, their accomplishments, and the accomplishments of their families. Display articles about students and their relatives on this bulletin board. Display pictures of the various classrooms in the school and lists of those students in that class. Each week or month focus on a different teacher and his class. Take several pictures of the teacher and the kids in action in the classroom and add to the display.

This bulletin board will serve as a place where the principal of the school can present an activity that can involve any student in the school who wishes to participate. Each month during the school year the principal creates an activity. Since the word *principal* has a homonym, what better activity to begin with than a homonym activity. Students could contribute homonym pairs to the board. The principal could announce a contest. Any student who submits a pair of homonyms that no one else submits wins a certificate or gets to participate in a special event. Through the year other focuses could include: unscrambling seasonal words, creating a school flag, an art contest, identifying leaves, entering a kite creation/flying contest, and creating a slogan for open house. Through this bulletin board the principal of the school, with minimum effort, gets involved with the students in a positive way.

Use this bulletin board to highlight the community workers in your school's neighborhood. Instruct each class to choose one and do a heart collage about that individual. Also, instruct teachers to have their classes write letters of thanks to the selected individuals. Add the hearts to the bulletin board.

The purpose of this bulletin board is to reward positive actions by students in the school. The names of students could be changed weekly. The bulletin board is not intended to focus on just academic achievement. There are many ways a student could brighten the school.

Flower Pattern:

At a faculty meeting create a list of ways a child could brighten a school. Create criteria for inclusion on this bulletin board. The faculty may simply decide to include each child in the school sometime during the school year.

Praise and positive recognition should result in better self-concepts and a more positive outlook toward the school and the learning experience. You may wish to use this bulletin board to give students with problems an extra boost. This small reward could be the catalyst for more positive behavior or more intense effort.

GIVE A HAND
FOR OUR SCHOOL'S WORKERS

Hand Pattern:

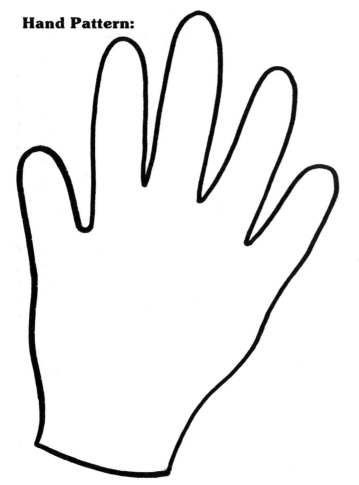

Use this bulletin board to say thanks, in a special way, to each of the workers who helps to make your school a success. Encourage each student to "adopt" one person who makes a specific contribution to your school. The student can get to know the person and prepare information about him for this bulletin board.

The librarian, special teachers, secretary, janitor, cook, bus driver, nurse, teachers' aids, helpful parents, and neighbors and friends of the school can be featured. After a person is featured, his name can be placed on a card or small hand and added to form a border for the bulletin board.

Use the hand pattern on the left to feature information about one of the school helpers. A photograph can be attached, as well as information about the person and a special thank-you note.

Use this bulletin board to feature a teacher. Give the teacher a much needed pat on the back. Encourage each student to design a thank-you card complete with illustration and verse for the teacher. The completed cards could be attached to the bulletin board. Develop a personal information form and ask the featured teacher to complete it. Post this on the bulletin board. Use an instant developing camera and take pictures of the teacher in action. You may also ask the teacher to furnish some photographs of family members and parents. Students would enjoy seeing a childhood picture of the teacher.

Emphasis could be placed on the other civic involvements of the teacher. Clubs he belongs to, organizations he participates in, and a brief history of the featured person's teaching career could be included.

The school's principal could write a letter of praise to the teacher, and this could be included in the material shown. Care should be taken to be sure this does not turn into a contest. Each teacher in the school should be featured. Names could be drawn at random, and the board could be continued until each teacher has been featured.

Many times students do not have the opportunity to see the teacher in any way but as seen in the classroom. The bulletin board will help all teachers to be multi-dimensional in the students' eyes.

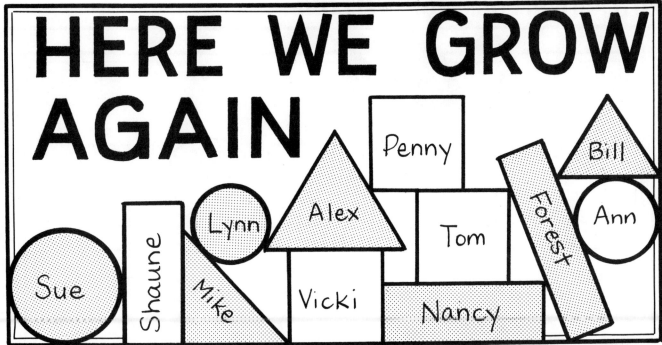

HERE WE GROW AGAIN

Use this bulletin board to welcome new students, teachers, and personnel to your school. Each time a new student or person joins your school, have him add a geometric construction paper shape to the bulletin board. The person should print his name on the shape. Have several construction paper shapes of various colors available. The newcomer can choose the shape and color. You may wish to print the following on each shape:

WE WELCOME _____ FROM _____ TO OUR SCHOOL.

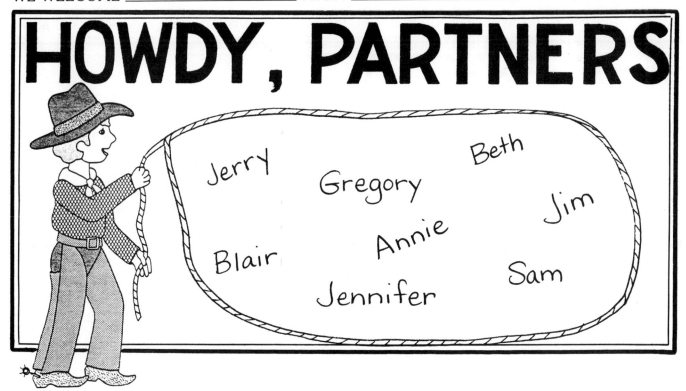

HOWDY, PARTNERS

This bulletin board can be created for the beginning of the school year. Each student's name and each employee's name should be included. Use a variety of colors of markers to print the names. Have the cowboy ask questions. These questions could include: Can you find your name? What is the most common name? These questions could be changed every few days.

Everyone loves to see his picture. Recognition is a positive force in a good self-concept. Each day as the students arrive, choose one or two students. Walk up to them with an instant developing camera and say "cheese." Put developed pictures on the bulletin board. The child's name should also be printed and placed by his name.

Cheese Pattern:

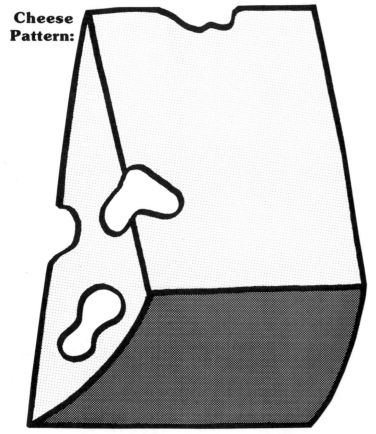

It won't take long for this bulletin board to become a popular spot in your school. Anticipation will grow. Children will wonder, will this be my day?

When the board is full, continue the process by taking down the picture that has been there the longest and replacing it with·today's new photo.

Candid pictures will create the most anticipation. If you choose to, the photos could be taken at any time during the school day.

The cafeteria line would be a great place to put this bulletin board. Most children will pass this spot at least once during the day.

Frog Pattern:

This bulletin board could be used to welcome new students to your school. After registration forms have been completed, print the new student's name on a frog pattern and allow the newcomer to pin it on the bulletin board.

A second purpose of this bulletin board could be to give recognition to students who attend the school. For no reason at all, print a child's name on a construction paper frog and attach it to the bulletin board. Then, sit back and watch the child's eyes light up when he discovers his name on the bulletin board.

In the spring use rabbits instead of frogs.

BE A PACESETTER!

MRS. LETTS GRADE 3

MRS. WIGHT GRADE 3

Use this bulletin board to motivate students in a schoolwide effort to collect newspapers for the school's paper sale. Refer to the pattern below and make a turtle for each classroom. Identify it with the teacher's name and grade level represented. Place it on the left side of the bulletin board. Each time a classroom collects a specific amount, has 100% participation, or displays a class effort for the good of the school, the turtle advances. Turtles can advance for additional reasons besides the paper sale. For example, if the class helped clean up the school grounds, they could advance. Perhaps each class could choose a project to complete. The schoolwide goal would be to reach the opposite side of the bulletin board and set the pace for progress. Accomplishments could be printed on flags and pinned to the bulletin board display.

Turtle Pattern:

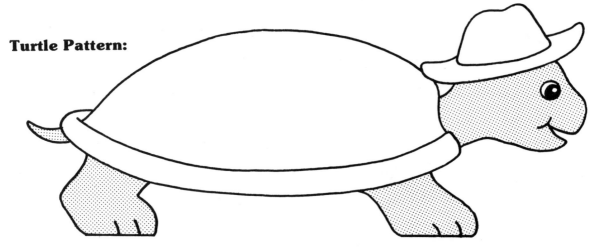

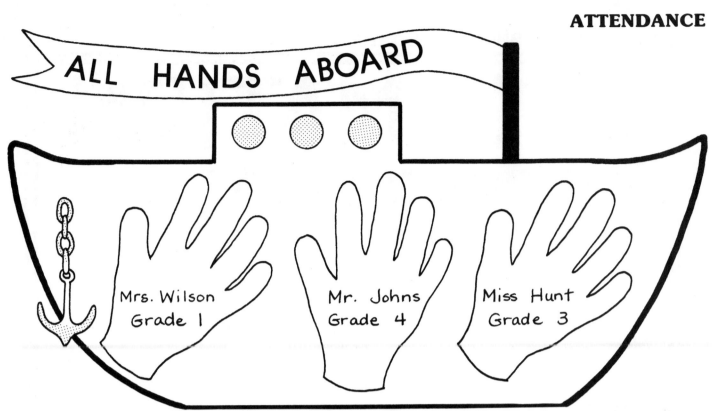

Use this bulletin board to promote good attendance. Each time a class has perfect attendance for a week, allow the class to place a hand (traced from one of the students) on the board. Print the teacher's name and the grade level on the hand. The goal of this display is to entirely fill the ship with hands.

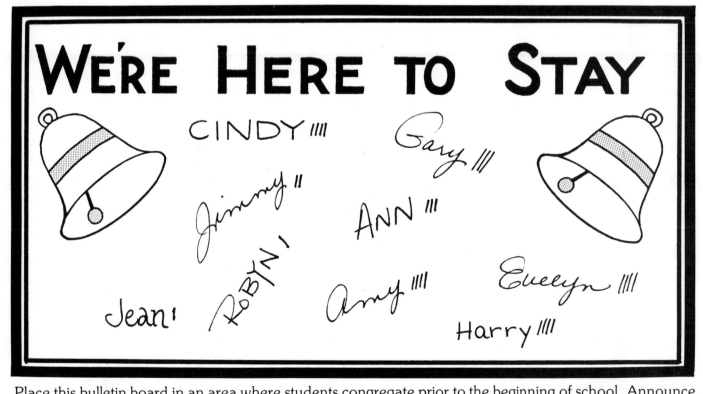

Place this bulletin board in an area where students congregate prior to the beginning of school. Announce to all students in the school that each day they should "sign in." Provide a variety of colors of markers for students to use to complete this bulletin board activity. Instead of printing or writing his name each time, a student can simply make a mark after his name.

INFORMATION STATION

Use this bulletin board as an information station for the entire school. If put in a central location, all students can be informed of events that are taking place. Teachers and parents can also use this bulletin board as a source of information. Only one engine will be needed. You may wish to duplicate several cars. Each car should be dated. When that date has passed, the car can be removed and the remaining cars moved closer to the engine. In addition to the announcement of school functions, you may wish to include lists of afterschool activities. Community happenings of interest could be included, as well as worthwhile television programs. You could also include a car for weekend happenings.

Train Compartment Pattern:

Train Car Patterns:

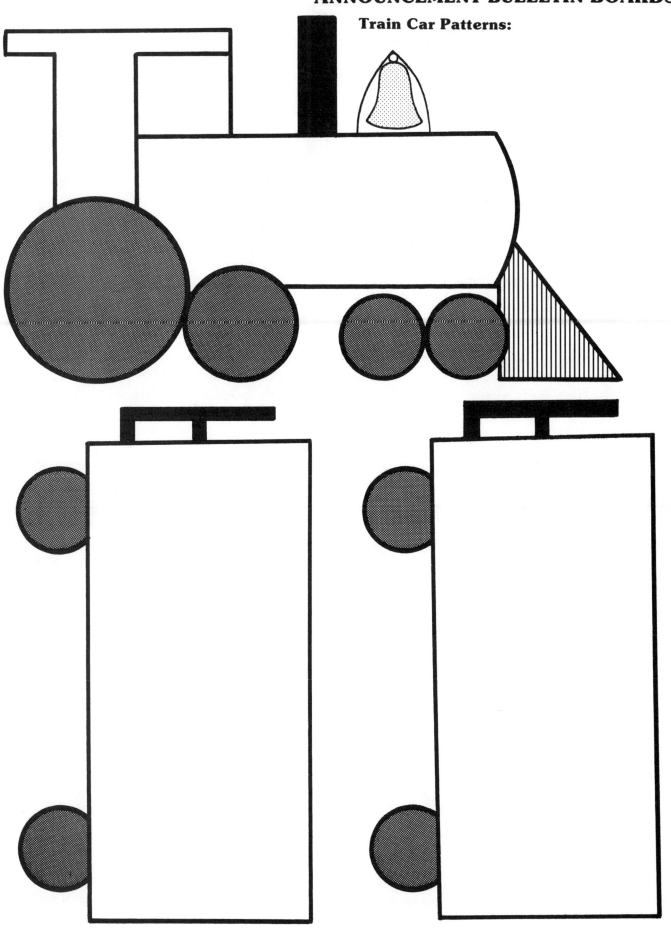

ANNOUNCEMENT BULLETIN BOARDS

Here is a bulletin board that can be used to display announcements of special interest to your students. Many times Scout leaders, dance instructors, 4-H leaders, etc., ask to have flyers passed out or displayed. Here is just the place for such announcements.

The theme of this bulletin board is quite similar to the one above. But it will bring a welcome change and can be used to renew interest in announcements. You may wish to use various colors of paper and markers to make a more attractive display. A stack of paper and some markers can be ready to give to anyone wishing to print an announcement. This will create a more uniform and neater display.

This board and the one to the left can be used where space is limited to create the same effect of the bulletin board shown above. Enlarge the bird pattern and use construction paper to make birds of several colors. Each bird can carry a notice of interest to the students. Many times announcements of limited interest are given over a school's intercom system. Use the bulletin boards on this page to relay messages of limited appeal. No use boring students with unrelated messages.

Use this bulletin board to display information of interest to the students of your school. The information could be announcements. However, this bulletin board could be used to inform your students of interesting happenings, news items, and general information on a variety of topics. Two or three pieces of information at one time would be sufficient. You may choose to present the same information in three levels, one for primary students, one for intermediate students, and one for gifted readers. At World Series time, present interesting information about the history of the event. The topics could range from A (aerobics) to Z (zoological parks).

The purpose of this bulletin board is not to provide details. It is designed to provide just the basic information about an upcoming event. The name of the event, the date, and the time is about all there would be room for. For example, NO SCHOOL, Tuesday the 15th, Teachers' Workshop! Basketball Game—Wednesday the 10th—4:00.

Use this bulletin board to publicize events that are taking place in your school or accomplishments achieved by school members. Write the information on stars and add them to the bulletin board.

Use this bulletin board to display important events that will be taking place at your school.

Use this bulletin board in a variety of ways to present information to your students. Enlarge the stoplight pattern found to the right. Make three signs. One should say STOP, the second should say CAUTION, and the third should say GO. You will also need a red, a yellow, and a green construction paper circle for your stoplight. Display the correct sign and the appropriate color of construction paper at the same time.

Stoplight Pattern:

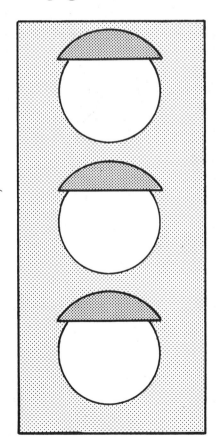

STOP!   School will be dismissed at 2:30 on Thursday.

CAUTION!   Running in the hall could cause an accident.

GO!   Basketball game on Wednesday. The team needs your support.

STOP!   Field trip tickets on sale now in the office.

CAUTION!   Book rental fees must be paid by Friday.

GO!   The public library will have a story hour at 10:00 on Saturday the 22nd.

Use this basic bulletin board theme year-round in a variety of clever ways. Refer to the tree pattern found on the next page, and enlarge and laminate it. This tree can be recycled each month by changing the shapes that are added to the tree. Each month a different classroom could be in charge of decorating the tree and creating a title for the wall/bulletin board display. The making of the decorations could be a terrific art project in which each student could participate. Titles could include "Tree-Mendous Fun for All," "A Tree-Mendously Bright Idea," or "A Tree for All Occasions." Here are some suggestions for decorating the tree.

Pattern for "A Tree for All Seasons":

CONDUCT / MANNERS

This bulletin board can encourage good conduct. From the pattern below make an arrow for each classroom. Identify the arrow by printing the teacher's name and grade level on it. Place completed arrow on the left side of the bulletin board. Each time a class as a whole displays excellent behavior, advance the arrow toward the apple on the right side of the board. A pattern to use in making the apples is on the right. The goal, of course, is to be the first class to reach the apple. The reward for the winning class—a crisp, crunchy, juicy, red apple.

Apple Pattern:

Arrow Pattern:

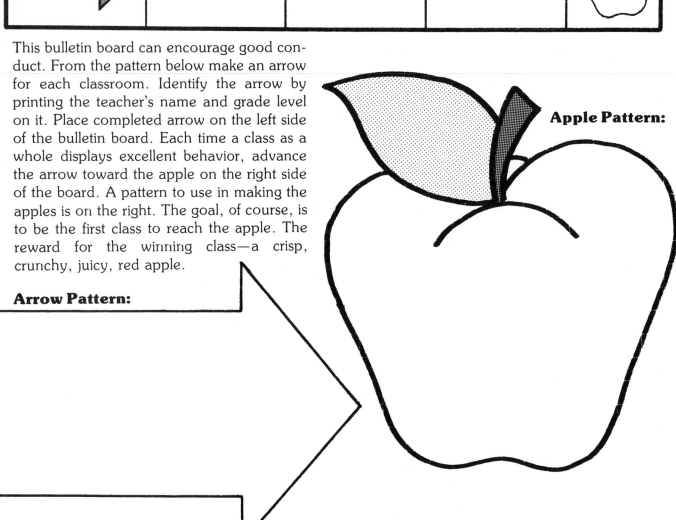

22

ROOT FOR GOOD MANNERS

Football Pattern:

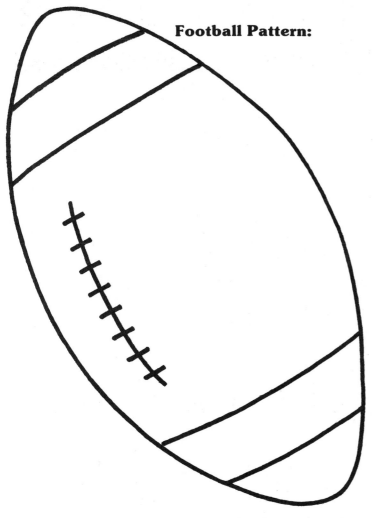

Use this bulletin board to encourage good manners. Use the football pattern to the left and make one for each classroom. Print each teacher's name and the grade level on a football. Each time a student shows good manners, instruct the teacher to allow the child to place a star on the football.

During the winter months, basketballs can replace the footballs. In the spring, tennis balls could be used.

From time to time you may wish to print a good manner rule on a piece of paper and attach it to the bulletin board. Some examples are:
Say please and thank you.
Excuse yourself when leaving the table.
Excuse yourself if you bump into someone.
Don't talk while chewing.

Use this bulletin board to encourage students to work together and to cooperate. Each student that displays such behavior should print his name on a construction paper ribbon made from the pattern below. These can be pinned to the bulletin board area to form a border.

This bulletin board can be used for several weeks if the wording on the sign is changed each week. Several suggestions about togetherness and cooperation can be made. Let's pull together to . . .

Have a Safe School
Beat East School (in softball)
Help the Needy

Promote School Spirit
Clean Up the Playground
Support Our School

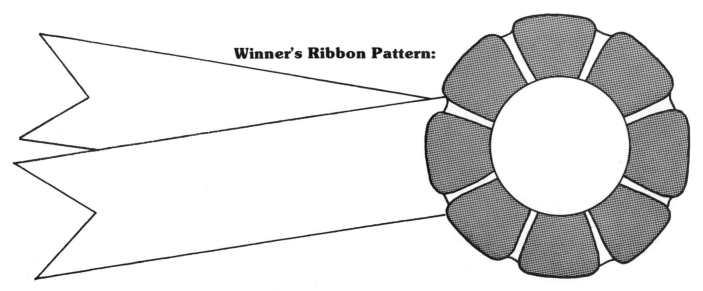

Winner's Ribbon Pattern:

Other titles for this bulletin board might include: "Our School Has a Clean Team," "Our Scene's a Clean Scene," and "Let's Make a Clean Sweep." You may wish to display just the illustration to this bulletin board and have a school contest to see who can create the best slogan, or do just the reverse. Create the title from construction paper letters and allow students to design illustrations for this bulletin board.

Encourage all students to help keep the school neat and clean with this bulletin board. On unannounced days, inspect the classrooms for neatness. This could be done just after school is dismissed. Determine which classroom is the neatest. On a construction paper boxing glove, print the name of the teacher and the grade level of that class. Pin the boxing glove to the bulletin board. This will give recognition to those students who try a little harder to be neat and tidy.

MOTIVATION

"Don't Let School Stump You" is a bulletin board designed to reinforce basic study and learning habits. From time to time, even the best students need to be reminded. In addition to the "tips" displayed on the board above, the following could be included: ask questions, pay attention, try your best, ask for help, be polite, use your time well, read carefully, think, get proper rest, come prepared, check your work, and have a set time for homework. Change the "tips" occasionally to keep interest. Ask students to volunteer additional ideas.

"Tools for School," the bulletin board illustrated above, is a simple one to create. Cover the board with a bright background paper, cut the title letters from a contrasting color of construction paper, and attach actual tools or pictures of tools the students will need for school. Number each item, scramble the letters that spell its name and ask the students to keep a list of all items displayed. From time to time take an item down and replace it until about a dozen tools have been displayed. Give a pencil to each student who turns in a correctly spelled list of all the items that were displayed.

On this page you will find two bulletin boards that encourage students to do their best. " 'Elf' You're Smart, You'll Study" projects this important message and will make a dull hall wall brighter. To change this bulletin board so it can be used longer, change the word study to pay attention, listen, work hard, try, be here, etc.

On the "handle" cards shown on the bulletin board "Be a Good Buddy, Be Sure to Study," print good study habits: read carefully, think, ask questions, work in a quiet place, go to the library, don't waste work time, and proof your paper are among the messages that can be displayed.

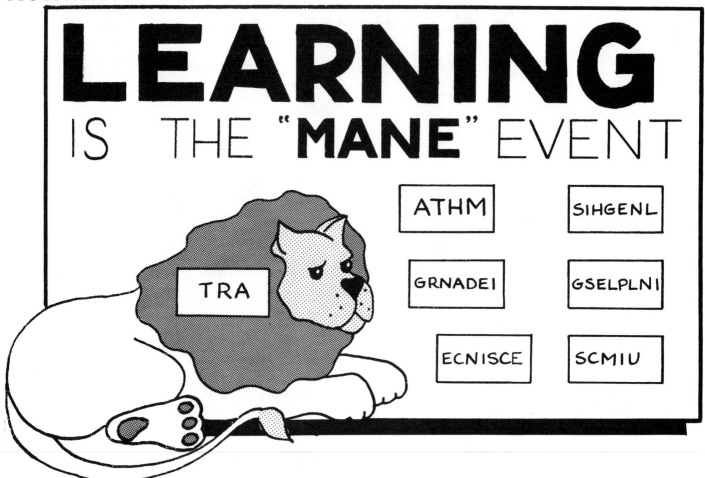

Use this bulletin board to focus on the importance of learning about a wide variety of topics. On index cards, scramble the names of subjects that are studied in school. Encourage students to maintain a list of the topics presented. This bulletin board can be used a long time by recycling. Each week a different teacher could be responsible for creating the list of scrambled words. In addition to a general list of subjects, specific lists for various subjects could be presented. Several lists are presented below.

Social Studies	**Math**	**Language**	**Science**
maps	addition	words	animals
people	subtraction	sentences	plants
places	multiplication	punctuation	planets
events	division	synonyms	nature
countries	fractions	capitalization	energy
history	graphs	vocabulary	weather
landforms	measuring	poetry	insects

If you choose to use lists similar to those above, retitle the bulletin board to say "Learning Is the 'Mane' Event in Science," etc. You may have some students in your school who would like to contribute lists for this bulletin board. A student should be encouraged to create a list of words on a specialized topic.

TREASURES AWAIT YOU IN SCHOOL

There are two ways to use the above bulletin board. First, the treasure chest could be stuffed with book jackets, learning tools, index cards that have topics printed on them, or pictures of students learning in various areas of the building. A second way this bulletin board can be used is to place several construction paper pencils on the board. On each pencil should be printed a short message.

The above bulletin board will make an attractive display for your school. Similar titles pertaining to transportation could include, "School Is a Place for TRAIN-ing," "You AUTO Try to Do Your Best," "Your Knowledge Is BALLOON-ing," and "All Aboard for Learning Fun."

This bulletin board is designed to involve everyone in the school. The purpose is cooperation and to visually see what one million looks like. The task is to create one million of something. You may decide to collect pop tops, bottle tops, dried beans, or make hash marks. Several ways to create one million will be described below.

COLLECTING POP TOPS: Pop tops and bottle caps seem to be quite plentiful, but can one million of them be found? Have the students begin collecting, counting, and bundling. Each one hundred pop tops can be tied together with a piece of string. This can be pinned to the bulletin board. Each one hundred bottle caps can be placed in a small plastic bag and closed with a bit of string. These can also be pinned to the bulletin board. Each time 10,000 tops have been pinned to the bulletin board, they should be taken down and piled in a large box. A star can be placed on the bulletin board to indicate that 10,000 more have been collected.

COLLECTING DRIED BEANS AND PEAS: Each 1,000 pieces of dried beans can be securely tied in a baggie. These bags can be attached to the bulletin board. Just 1,000 bags full will equal the million.

MAKING HASH MARKS: Perhaps the easiest way to create a million is to make hash marks on index cards. Each card could hold 1,000 marks or ten lines of one hundred. Each child in the school could contribute his share. The completed cards could be displayed on the bulletin board and continued in a line down the hall and around the school until a total of one million has been reached.

TERRIFIC TIP: Have a chart posted next to the bulletin board and each time a class makes a contribution, instruct them to make a mark by the appropriate name. A graph could be created to show progress.

Involvement in this project could take place over an extended period of time. Many opportunities for math projects will exist, but best of all, the entire school will be working together toward a goal.

For a simple and purposeful bulletin board, place a blank map of the United States on a bulletin board. Title the bulletin board "Where Did You Go Last Summer?" The letters for the title can be cut from various colors of construction paper. Encourage the students of your school to complete the bulletin board.

1. Let each student place a star on the map to indicate the location of his vacation.
2. Use a pin to attach a piece of yarn to the star.
3. At the other end of the yarn, off the map, the student should place a card naming the place visited.
4. A postcard or a picture of the student's choice could be pinned next to the name.
5. Some students may also want to pin a memento from the trip next to the sign.

ADDITIONAL IDEAS:

Collect postmarks from envelopes and glue them to the map of the United States in the proper locations. The goal could be to completely cover the map with postmarks.

Students could bring in articles from various cities and communities in the United States. Use the articles as the bulletin board's border and print the names of the cities and communities in various colors of marker to make a colorful map.

The bulletin board could focus on the cities where professional baseball, football, and hockey teams are located. Each team's nickname could be printed where the city is located. Students could identify the name of each city.

ADDITIONAL TITLES:

Where Were You Born?	State Birds
Where Do Your Grandparents Live?	Famous Landmarks
Where Would You Like to Visit?	Historical Happenings

Everyone in the school can contribute to the creation of this bulletin board. Have each person trace his hand and print his name on it. Assign each class red, white, or blue, and have them make the hands in that color. A large American flag can be created by assembling the hands in the proper places. Choose an appropriate place for this display, such as the wall of the gym, cafeteria, or hall.

TERRIFIC TIP: Be sure to plan this bulletin board display very carefully, and make a preliminary drawing. Add up the total hands you will have prior to assembling them, and arrange them in equal rows to be sure you will have enough to complete the overall flag.

UNSCRAMBLE THE DOGS

LOCILE 3.

RPENIOT 4.

PLODEO 1.

DOHUN 5.

GEBLAE 2.

RETRIRE 6.

Use the bulletin boards on this page to present clever contests to your students. A different contest could be presented each month. "Unscramble the Dogs" would be a contest for unscrambling words. Place pictures of different breeds of dogs on the bulletin board. Scramble the letters of each breed's name by the picture. Place an empty dog biscuit box on the board for students to put their unscrambled answers in. Refer to the *Golden Book of Dogs* for some unusual breeds to display.

CREATE A SCHOOL FLAG

Challenge your students to design and make from construction paper flags for your school. Add the paper flags to the display. Let students vote. Have the winning flag created from cloth and permanently display it at your school.

THE GREATEST LIVING ★AMERICAN★

During the month of February, have each student enter a theme writing contest on the individual he feels is the greatest living American. Invite a community member to help judge the essays, and let the students' work be published in your school's newsletter. Display the completed themes.

STUDENTS
✦✦✦✦IN THE NEWS✦✦✦✦

NAME:
JUSTIN SPIZMAN

BORN:
JANUARY 18, 1981

Create a bulletin board to resemble your local newspaper. Each week a different student could be featured. Let the student be responsible for the bulletin board. Students could add pictures of their families, friends, pets, etc. The background of this bulletin board could be covered with newspaper and the details pinned in place.

ADDITIONAL IDEAS:

Teachers could be featured on the bulletin board. School workers could also be the focus.

OUR COMMUNITY IN THE NEWS: The community's happenings could also be highlighted and presented in newspaper form. Refer to your community newspaper for interesting articles and stories that would interest students. Invite a neighborhood reporter to talk to your class about his job and about how the newspaper is created.

GOOD NEWS — BAD NEWS: Divide this bulletin board in half, and instruct students to bring in articles about the school or community. Add the good news to the good side and the bad news to the bad side. Encourage students to keep this bulletin board updated with current events.

THIS WEEK'S NEWS: Each week a different classroom could be responsible for the creation and continuation of this bulletin board.

ADDITIONAL TIPS: Try to get a variety of newspapers from other cities. Cover the bulletin board background with the pages, and encourage students to try to identify the location of each page by reading its contents. The pages could be numbered, and students could record their findings.

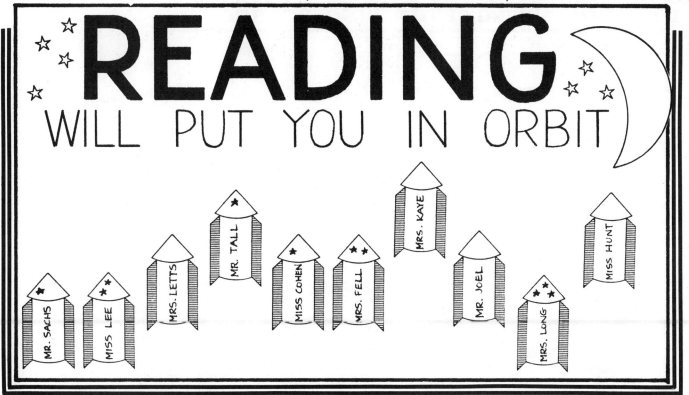

Use this bulletin board to encourage students to read more books and to visit the library. Each time a class visits the library during the school year, advance the rocket upward one or two inches. The first rocket to reach the moon (having turned in all their checked-out books) receives a special treat. Treats could include a story hour created especially for the class. Refer to the rocket pattern below and make one for each class.

*A star could be awarded each week a class does not have an overdue book.

Rocket Pattern:

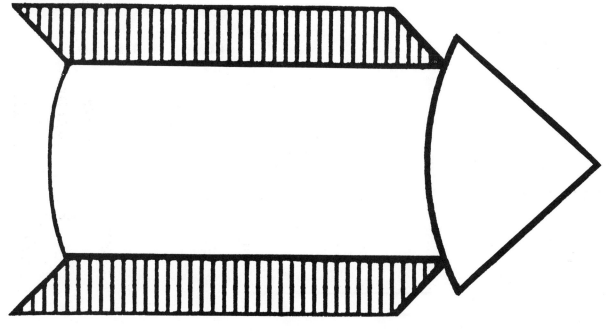

Hat Pattern:

Use this bulletin board in the library to motivate students to read more books and to visit the library more often. From the hat pattern on the left, make as many hats as needed so that there is one hat per class. Each time a student from a class visits the library and checks out a book, allow him to paste a star to the class's hat.

TERRIFIC TIP: Another way to use this bulletin board is to label the hats to focus on various types of books that can be found in the library (mystery, biography, animal story, western, travel). Place corresponding book jackets behind the top of each hat, showing just enough of the cover to entice the readers who visit the library.

Use this bulletin board to motivate students to read more books and to visit the library.

TERRIFIC TIP: Use ready-made book jackets on this bulletin board, and change them daily.

A rocket pattern can be found on page 35. Students will enjoy contributing planets and spacecrafts made from construction paper to this bulletin board.

An alternate title for this bulletin board could be "Feed Your Mind—Digest a Book." Book jackets can be placed on real paper plates. Have students bring in some fancy ones left over from a recent cookout or party. Other titles could be "Spoon Up Some Interesting Reading," "Books Worth Biting Into," "Munch a Mystery," or "Reading Is Food for Thought."

Use this bulletin board to promote enthusiasm for the library. Book jackets or titles of books for students to read can be displayed on the balloons. After a student has read a specific number of books, a balloon could be given as a special treat.

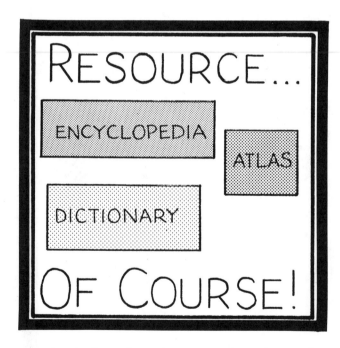

Use this bulletin board to present to the students the variety of resource/reference books that are available to them. Print the name of the resource book on a piece of construction paper. Below in smaller letters, print some of the types of information that the book contains.

Let your students vote for a favorite book each week or each month. Display the book's jacket under a construction paper magnifying glass. Add interest by making the center of the magnifying glass from a piece of plastic laminating film or cellophane. More than one book could be displayed.

ALL SORTS OF SPORTS

Use this bulletin board to introduce students to the variety of activities that relate to physical education. Encourage students to collect magazine and newspaper articles on the various sports and add them to the bulletin board to inform their fellow students. Place pictures on the board. Number each one and have students guess the name of each sport from the picture. Change pictures until a total of twenty sports has been shown. Students submit completed entries. Each winner receives a paper trophy.

Use this bulletin board in physical education to motivate students to achieve a goal you specify for them to reach. As each student reaches the goal, allow him to add a first place ribbon with his name on it to the bulletin board. Goals could include a specific number of laps to run, good behavior, good listening skills during class, or good sportsmanship. Refer to page 24 and duplicate the ribbon pattern for this bulletin board.

Use this bulletin board to display any and all information that reflects the physical education program in your school. Items that could be displayed include: the standings and records of the school's sports teams or intramural teams, the won/lost records of teams, and sports-related articles. Other ideas that would relate to this bulletin board could be added, and the P.E. teacher, school secretary, or principal could maintain it.

ADDITIONAL IDEAS:

1. Students could draw illustrations of the school's mascot.

2. Photos from games could be taken and displayed on this bulletin board.

3. Newspaper clippings of the coverage of the team could be added.

4. A border could be added to this board. Items could be construction paper replicas of the equipment used in various sports.

5. Terms/Words used in the various sports could be defined or presented for students to become familiar with. Here are some examples.

technical	time out	defense	overtime
free throw	jump shot	offense	official

6. Scramble the letters used to spell various athletic activities. Number each scrambled word and let students try to pin the letters in the correct order.

7. Print three words that relate to a sport. The students must guess the sport.

a. love, let, advantage	tennis
b. eagle, flag, wedge	golf
c. jib, current, catamaran	sailing
d. defense, I-formation, pads	football
e. camel, sit-spin, rink	figure skating

Use this bulletin board to encourage good health habits. Make as many hearts as you will need from the pattern below. Print a good health practice on each heart. Let this bulletin board stress taking care of your vision, your teeth, etc.

Heart Pattern:

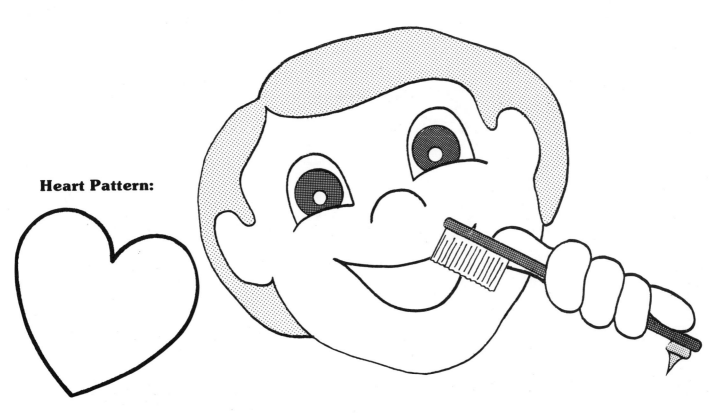

HIP, HIP HOORAY FOR THE P.T.A.

Mrs. Gates
Mrs. John

Mrs. Bell
Mrs. Katz

Mrs. Sands
Mrs. Hunt

Hippo Pattern:

Use this bulletin board to encourage schoolwide participation in the P.T.A. From the pattern on the left, make a hippo for each classroom. Each time a parent of a student in that class joins your school's P.T.A., have the teacher of that class add the parent's name to the hippo. When a class reaches 100%, complete participation, add a bow or ribbon to the hippo. This board could also be used to announce P.T.A. meetings, projects, and accomplishments.

TEACHER'S PETS

Use this bulletin board to display artwork created by students. Have an art lesson where students make animals from construction paper. Encourage students to refer to pictures of the real animals and try to be "realistic" in the details. Add the finished "works of art" to the bulletin board.

Other titles that could be used to display student artwork include: "I Was Framed," "A Gallery of Good Art," or "Got a Hang-Up" (this one could have a clothesline and the art could be displayed on T-shirts hanging on the line).

ART IN ACTION

DISPLAY ACTION PICTURES HERE

Use this bulletin board to display paintings created by students on the theme of action. Instruct each student to paint a picture of himself in action doing something he likes to do. Ideas could include a sport, a hobby, raking leaves, etc.

SCHOOL WAS GOOD
TO THE LAST DROP

Raindrop Pattern:

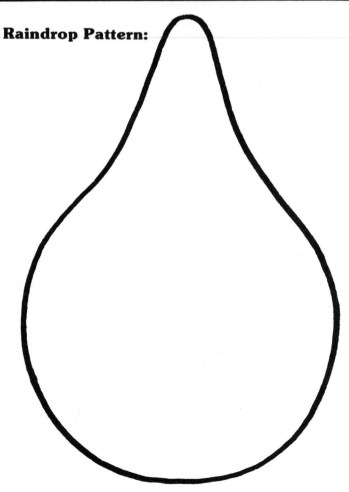

Use this bulletin board at the end of the school year to highlight the school year's events. Make as many raindrops as you will need and add them to the bulletin board. On each raindrop place a photograph or memorabilia that depicts an event that took place during the school year.